Hortensia,

in winter

Megan

Merchant

newamericanpress
✳
Milwaukee, Wisconsin

n e w a m e r i c a n p r e s s
✻
Milwaukee, Wisconsin

Hortensia, in winter
© 2024 BY MEGAN MERCHANT

Printed in the United States of America
ISBN 978-1-941561-33-1

Cover + Book Design by Angelo Maneage

For ordering information, please contact:
INGRAM BOOK GROUP
ONE INGRAM BLVD.
LA VERGNE, TN 37086
(800) 937-8000
ORDERS@INGRAMBOOK.COM

For media and event inquiries, please visit:
WWW.NEWAMERICANPRESS.COM

PROUD MEMBER
[clmp]

Hortensia,

in winter

Megan

Merchant

Hortensia, in winter

"'I am looking for the word that falls between almost and touch. That consideration. It has its own airspace,' writes Merchant in the poem 'Exodus.' It is precisely this consideration that ruffles the airspace between, and within, the poems of *Hortensia, in winter*; a languorous, circular journey into lineage and inheritance. Among the many voices in this collection is Hortensia, for whom the book is named, and whom the speaker addresses directly in a series of epistolary prose poems. 'I am growing my hair longer than our bloodline,' she writes. 'I am braiding it as a rope to reach you.' This reaching does not begin with Hortensia nor does it end with the speaker. It is whispered into the corners of history so as to be heard on the other side. 'Here, the rooms of the body are ravaged by fingerprints & feathers.' To spend time with this book is to consider this body's lament, to listen to the silences that shorten the distance between almost and touch."

JAMAICA BALDWIN, AUTHOR OF *BONE LANGUAGE*

"What does it mean to be 'given the smallest room in the house of your own life?' This collection expertly explores this theme, in unforgettable poems about ancestry, family, and the remarkable struggle of motherhood and womanhood. In exquisite language, the poet Megan Merchant asks the essential questions such as 'what happens when light reaches the unsayable.' But say it, she must, as we journey through Hortensia's world and beyond. On this road we find bones and chapped prayers, radishes in a white bowl, chokecherry, lilac and maple. 'To sink into the earth is a gift' just as it is to sink into each poem, each brilliant work. In each line, we will find layers of meaning and 'words that will peel the generations between us.'"

CONNIE POST, AUTHOR OF *BETWEEN TWILIGHT* AND *BROKEN METRONOME*

"'What have I become that wasn't already weft into the cloth of my story?' asks the speaker of Megan Merchant's *Hortensia, in winter*, a speaker weary and untethered after decades of trying to please: 'I forgot where to place the beginning—how I broke on the back porch, never told a soul.' In these artfully crafted poems, Merchant seeks understanding of the uneasy present by pulling on a thread linking to the past—Mormon ancestor Hortensia. What the speaker finds as she follows that thread is an 'echo in a tunnel scrummed with graffiti'—ghosts of stories that can never be fully deciphered, proof of a journey whose secrets will never give themselves up entirely. Some histories can never be fully uncovered, not when 'women's voices weren't allowed to blaze and bright.' But there, in that enigmatic space of half-knowing, the speaker and Hortensia find one another. Hortensia may not surrender all the answers, but that cloth of her own story wraps around a speaker whose truthful, unsparing poems call to us all."

JESSICA WALSH, AUTHOR OF *BOOK OF GODS AND GRUDGES*

"*Hortensia, in winter* is an alluring exploration of bodies—familial and womanly and earthly. Some of the poems seem to want to escape themselves, shedding their pain like an exoskeleton or skin. Others remain a tangle of ache, sites of historical and motherly ferocity. Some read like dialogues across time—woman to ancestor to son— the vacillations between them ethereal and earth-bound, a strand of Mormon history woven throughout. I found myself wanting to linger inside every exquisitely crafted prose poem housed within its pages."

ROSEMARIE DOMBROWSKI, POET LAUREATE OF PHOENIX, AZ

"In a letter to her cousin, Emily Dickinson once wrote, 'We must be careful what we say. No bird resumes its egg.' Megan Merchant, in these attentive, interrogative, and enduring poems, realizes the difficult act of naming the tensions between desire and faith. A series of epistles to her ancestor,Hortensia, in winter is a 'testimony of wreckage' that challenges the enduring and patriarchal constraints of life in a woman's body. A symphony of birds and the pressing cold of coming winter bear down on Merchant's fine-tuned acts of apostasy. This book is an invocation to anima mundi, an act of resistance against linear time. *Hortensia, in winter* leaves me shimmering with a kind of ache 'more rabid than hunger'."

JENNY MOLBERG, PH.D, AUTHOR OF *THE COURT OF NO RECORD,* EDITOR OF *PLEIADES*

I

II

My blood is alive with many voices telling me
I am made of longing.

R.M. RILKE

I'm a ghost of you, you're a ghost of me...

GREGORY ALAN ISAKOV, SAN LUIS

THERE CAME TO MAGNOLIA, IOWA, IN 1852, by way of Kanesville, Lucius Merchant and his wife Hortensia, who out in the exodus of 1846 with one son, Amasa who with the others of the posterity still reside in this locality. In order to make the matter herein related more potent we will say that the name and life of Lucius and Hortensia Merchant were without blame, souls of honor, known in all the country in pioneer days and until their death, both within and without the church, as the very best people, quiet, unassuming, yet steadfast and true not only in the church, but in home and society. An incident expressive of this we give as told by a Mr. G, who purchased a home and farm near Magnolia, in 1877. Mr. G said that Mr. Hillis (father of Reverend Newell Dwight Hillis) from whom he purchased said, 'You will find Magnolia a nice place to live, with nice people, but it's a hotbed of Mormonism." Mr. G said, "I had never met any, and from what I had heard of them, I expected to be able to tell a Mormon on sight, so shortly after coming I needed seed wheat and was directed to Lucius Merchant. I found him very kind. He gave me big measure at reduced price. Being a stranger he did all to make me welcome. Dinner I must have. I enjoyed their company greatly. I came home and told my wife I had met a most excellent couple. Soon afterward, I was told they were Mormons. At first thought it staggered me, and I wondered if the wheat would grow...

ALMA FREYANDO,
"TESTIMONY OF THE PAST: AS A VOICE FROM THE DEAD"

HORTENSIA, BORN MARCH 30, 1824. Her parents were Henry and Lucy. Her father had owned a small silk mill in Hopedale, Mass and later in Bedford. Her parents practically died after her and her bother Rufus joined Joseph Smith. We had letters from her to her parents telling how much she needed them, etc. but no reply. There's also the sad story of the murder of Joseph Smith and his brethren and how the whole settlement of thousands was forced to head further west. At this point, Joseph Smith's wife and young son assumed they were to take over but a strong leader under Smith, Brigham Young, announced that he was to be the new prophet.

1846, Mormons now under Brigham Young, were driven out of Nauvoo. Lucius and Hortensia parted from the church when polygamy was accepted as doctrine and joined the reorganized branch following Joseph Smith's widow. Then they left the trek west and farmed at Kanesville in 1851.

CARROLL MILTON MERCHANT

I

INVOCATION

I want to ask the hard questions, but they sharpen back to god. You drained a swamp by digging ditches that fed the Mississippi. Fired red bricks and felt the sweat of oxen laboring. What do I know about this life that wasn't built on your foundation? My grandfather's great-grandmother, you've found me, hands too cold for a needle to puncture my paper-thin veins. I'm wrecked. I'm closed into a winter that doesn't answer. All bones and chapped prayers. Maybe I found you. Maybe the only thing that matters is what comes after the last word.

DEAR HORTENSIA,

(March 1824-April 1905)

Did they bring a cat into the corner of the room when you birthed, to teach you how to clamp down complaint? You are ancestor and glyph. A hemline soaked wet in shit and faith. I wind a thread around my finger until it numbs to try and understand what it must have been like—the feral winter, a crown of unanswered prayers, emptiness unkempt. To dream of apples and grow thin on nothing but god. To house a passion in the rooms of your body more rabid than hunger. You should know—the coyotes yip your name here, in dark. They are applying for sainthood. In the morning, I remove a juniper log that refused to burn. Bury it with what wasn't snared—bone bits, apple core, a marrow of dark hair. Untamed.

HELPMEET:

to make man "comfortable...to dress his food...be
pleasing to his sight, and...be in all respects...entirely
answerable to his...wants and wishes."

JOHN GILL, 18-CENTURY BIBLICAL SCHOLAR

There are days I feel porous. Drool paint through a tea strainer
onto linen. Others, I walk the dog, plunge stones in the
creek with insults. To be all things at once while still being
yourself—isn't that the goal? Hortensia, were you given the
smallest room in the house of your own life? I am gifted a
single window. Winter crammed in the way that only a cat
could skuttle through. You are my periscope, the law of
reflection at play, these poems—the surface. Teach me how
to dismantle desire. The roots of it. *De sidere,* meaning *from
the stars.* I hear deciduous—*the dropping of a part that is no longer
needed or useful.* Chokecherry, lilac, maple. At the first bend of
cold, I imagine the small flush of your garden plot in bloom,
how such tedious keeping was meant to bring delight, only to
wake each morning and find it flooded with flightless birds.

EVERY DAY I DRAW A DIFFERENT BIRD,

a heron—lanky, keen on watching, from a far-bank. The crow
not swept behind, whispers things I was always meant to recall,
but have shed—how to make a slipknot from a bra strap, how
to uncork a bottle with a stone, gut a fish with an ink stain.
The ravens—bend light. Bats tendril the load bearing walls of
my chest. They are pockets secreted in night. Hummingbirds
teach me F minor. Then F minor breaks me apart. And
maybe the bird is the ache is the joint, and maybe it swallows
the room with flight even when it looks, from the window,
most like a cage. Or, maybe I am meant to sustain by envy—
the slurry of gnats that funnel from an empty can, the sweet
licked all-clean.

APPLYING FOR SAINTHOOD

My mother reached for the horse, to stroke the braided mane, pet instead the electric fence. *Jesus Christ.* This, I feared, all along, was her view of motherhood—tenderness scraped from the bone.

She kissed a single dot of blood, pressed it to the ground. *Anima mundi.* Promised me a four leaf clover would grow there.

    //

I was never precious, but constantly ill. Each fever, a beatitude, a prayer to the saint who fluttered the rafters. *Take her name,* she said, when age came & I had to attach my spirit to the church. I picked Elizabeth. She didn't last long.

    //

When the animals fell, it became Francis. We dug trenches for each damaged calf, each swatted bird. Plowed the forty acres with sweat. A woman's work, I was taught, was to endure.

    //

As her sight slipped, it became Helen, who sustained on holy bread. Helen of bones & hollows that would scare the ravens from the roof, looking already dead. My mother covered the horses' eyes with a veil.

//

Near the end, she moved to the foot of a mountain, yoked complaints to the wind. I still see her out at night, wracking up her list of curses, a fly swatter in hand, in case that mountain tries to fling them back. A woman must remain pure.

//

Hail Mary, body winged with claws, my husband is concerned because he hasn't heard my cry. I have been perched by the skunk body along the side of the road, slinging a pocket of colored glass at vultures, to learn how death brings delight. My mother never taught me her prayer for that—how to rip it clean, how to boil the bones and make a broth that sustains.

MERCIFUL

I meet with a surgeon to discuss a tubal ligation and think about the irrigation systems that flooded the acres of my youth. What grew there? Didn't I drive once, through a field of corn obscured by snow? Now, no daughter will seed. I will be scraped clean.

I sponge plates left for days in the sink. Nurturing. What have I become that wasn't already weft into the cloth of my story? When your letters were gifted into my hands, I knew I'd already traced your cursive into sleep. Hortensia, I write you back into being as if that's enough.

I dream of a dirt road where corn husk dolls litter the shoulder. What kind of monster feels relieved?

CONFINEMENT

I am told motherhood should be enough to keep me happy, and am asked to look in a mirror. Anger is a gift we are expected to secret. I collect burrs from the dead grass, let them hook my skirt in hopes of creating a defensible space, a few moments of quiet. I warm milk, sort socks, practice joy as if it is a thing to be fooled into, like love. A neighbor paints her car flat black, rams her mailbox backing out. Her anger is rearview. Mine winces ahead. I chase a raven from the roof, envy its wingspan. My husband complains that I can't hear my sons calling. They pull the red thread between us. So much mud heavies my boots, I leave them by the door. Facing out.

SEALING

silk sutures link us like marionettes / drips that freeze over
bark before descending / you can't hear the water's urge
unless it's rushing / you are my flood subject now / I scrub
a blue bowl in a chipped basin / drip my hair with lavender /
dream about sterile rooms / a salpingectomy / slender trunk
/ how did you carry, was it low / a diviner whispered my
daughters' names into my palms / a pit from a sweet rotted
fruit appeared under the juniper / *I would like to have one of your
early apples*, you wrote / was that prayer / on the coldest days
mountain lions grit their teeth outside my window / their
chatter sounds like church bells / after a hard freeze, did you
stand on the Mississippi and not think of drowning / your
nightgown floating white and clean as wind / did you listen

SUBJECTS TO CONSIDER FOR BOTH
PAINTING & WRITING

Film on my teeth after eating a hard-boiled egg. Why anyone would call blood *crimson*. Chopping wood on a day you can see your breath. The clicking sound that Mahjong tiles make. The speed at which they are placed. A windchime strung with bones. The way winter light feels most earnest in the morning. His chin, as it pressed against my shoulder blade. The muscles of grief that cramp without warning. Why men are allowed to age—the absence of a societal tantrum. The Farmer's Almanac that everyone in town is mumbling about. Radishes in a white bowl. Glue, hardened, on the window that looks like frost. Scratches on old records that are a kind of music. Gray hairs in the sink. How he unhooked the curtains and wrapped me, naked, in what light they still held.

PICKING WILD BERRIES

I spill bacon grease on the lawn, it shapes a perfect moon. Antlers hang on a wood paneled wall. A black and white tv sings with tin foil reception. The news is never good. Not everyone wants it to be. I dress in wool scarves stained with blackberries, they keep my collarbone warm enough some man could come close, snap a wish. Maybe I have memorized every constellation on the way out of town. I am learning the landscape of my lineage now because I can see the banks that cradle it—also, I'd like to find more than a name to hang in the rearview mirror.

A HOUSE OF MANIFESTOS

We use the fattest books to smash spiders, then open to page 49 and read. Anything can be bible, but I sleep with the book of *How to Survive Worst Case Scenarios* under my bed, a baggie of dry wall screws, and duct tape to hold us together. One article explains that you may feel more scattered than normal, unable to focus. I close my eyes, and see the spread of Northern Lights as hearts taped to neighbors' windows. This too is trauma response. Before she died, my mother made lists on yellow legal pads, so she would not forget how to operate the small machinery of her life. They feathered her cabinets and counters, heavily taped. How many times I've been told that a poem is simply the right words in the right order. I add eye bolts, sifted flour, scissors, salt.

THEY PROMISED THAT YOU WERE SET
APART FOR SOMETHING HOLY

Did you dream about oceans while you were mud-stuck in the Mississippi, something you couldn't see the banks of, like faith? Salt, birdwing, a weekday sneak of sour wine. You were all scripture and scrub oak, miracles that profited man. On Sundays, I open the dictionary, look for words you might have hummed, words that will peel the generations between us. Are your eyes hazel, do they shift in the onslaught of spring? The blue of needing another body to remind you of your own? Did you feel desire but give it your husband's name?

SELF-PORTRAIT AS A BURNED-OUT PORCH LIGHT

A tree crammed with bluebirds, snow. A forklift slips from a hill. The neighbor shoots his rifle to avalanche. A taste of rust. It's all a love poem. Even the owl's grief—how it spoons the dark. The open mouth of cold. I wanted it to be wistful. Forgive me, I am not telling this well. I forgot where to place the beginning—how I broke on the back porch, never told a soul. His eyes—smoked herring and blue. I plugged them into a different life. Then, morning. Garbage men collecting bins of dead birds, fish scales like glitter. Wax paper. String. An orchestra of leaving. I could never make sense of the way the trees glow, are backlit by kitchen windows, the silhouettes of wives in the dulled-quiet, scraping, rinsing, where they end and I

SCORE

Ravens scrounge trash from the neighbor's bin, then rise haphazard. The sunglow traces roofs and chimneys umber—a harbinger. What notes still play in my blood? What warnings? I imagine you looking at a fogged mirror, the shadow banks of the Mississippi, your husband's back rising and falling into sleep. A good wife. That's what holy means. I am all out of tune. When you had the choice to take a sister-wife, did you hear the alarm of ravens as A sharp minor—a triad not suitable for composition? Here, the ravens mimic a wolf's howl, draw them to a carcass, trick them into the tough work of tearing the flesh with their teeth, then dive.

FAMINE

A violin in the next room shames the silence that came before. Isn't that a kind of faith? Rustle something, if you are listening. Outside, winter is in a mood. It makes everything unclear. Even the birds are genuflecting. I take your silence as permission to continue.

PORTRAITURE: NUDE

We are taught to yearn for erasure. Red stockings drying over the porcelain tub. Strands of hair in the sink. The spot of shade between thighs. Pigeons on the landing, iridescent until the light rearranges, shifts to the apartment next-door, unpacks. If you were to paint *want* back into my skin, it would be with an old brush, streaks of morning blue stained into the bristles. The wood handle smooth, the air in the room tasting most like Spanish olives spooned directly from the can.

TABOO

After the monsoon welled against the house & the firing squad of hail dented every soft surface. After the falcons hurtled from cypress to cottonwood spotting prey & I woke thinking their cries were my son seizing in sleep. After the fear that I had lapsed in giving him meds & downed three glasses of screw top wine on the dark porch trying to remember the last place I'd seen myself, where I wasn't just the contrails of my debts, but the rind of music from the record player & cigarette perfume. After a friend said *the days are long, the years short* & I learned that desire is not a palindrome—it lurches at breakneck speed, then slips invisible like the snakes in our backyard pond that whisper into the chasm of rocks. All hiss & swallowing prey whole. After I learn that some female snakes have two clitorises in the shape of a heart, I put the rock down. Hortensia, how could I kill what is capable of deriving pleasure from this life?

RECKONING

A woman tells me she can warm her hands by ten degrees if she concentrates hard enough. I suffer into my body that is rarely above cold. Fingers clumsy as cicadas. Useless as hindsight. *We learn from our past,* my mother told me, but she too was untethered. *There are things we don't speak of here.* Which is why I go blank in the doctor's office when asked my history, why I have not attached myself to ailment as substrate, only displacement. Did you feel the presence before a temple had risen? In the arrowed wetland. Did you recognize that god was already homed as a feather, a pottered bowl, a burial site?

HYMN

I rouge. Melt salted butter in a dish as opaque as milk. When I went on a glass-bottom boat, I decided that you were my ghost. Sharp coral under the surface. If not for you, I would be someone's *Déjà vu*. But I am echo in a tunnel scrummed with graffiti. The bright script—handprints of the daughters that drowned in my body. You can name them, if you wish. They are, in some way, yours too. In my dreams, I am always teaching them how to swim.

PUTTING MY DEAD MOM'S DOG TO SLEEP

Fields of magnolia and sulfur. Fields of brick. Soft fur. Somewhere there is a horse leaning into shade, the dream of apples and mint cantering the air. A fallow of light. Damp honey and mold. Streaks of this world pressed to skin. I wash my hands under the pump, cold. Let the stains bleed into a wood bucket. Paint under my nails. Indigo. Soil. *Take a picture*, a friend urged, *of her death bed hands*. For when she is gone. Satin. Pinched laughter. Bone. They molded parts of me. The dog's fur holds the last stroke. A map of tuft, a canvas of ash.

NAUVOO, A TORNADO DEMOLISHED THE TEMPLE WALLS—1850

What rituals do we share? What omens? I know you baptize the dead. I arrange lilacs on a wood table, cover them with wax to keep. Wrap in rice paper and leave for those who come to share the word. They have to knock first, on a red door. Do the dead have any say? Because of the choices you made, I am free from everything except my anxiety. Were you also the understudy to yours? Did time, for you, have a fullness, or dwell?

"HAVE YOU BRANDED AN ANIMAL THAT YOU DID NOT KNOW TO BE YOUR OWN?"

The desert we drive through is not oasis but glistering sand and coyote muzzle from the window. When we trek home, I'm told not to look at rabbit entrails my husband wipes onto a shovel for a creek bed burial. A gift waiting at our door. Will I hear it in night, a commencement of pain? I sneak back out, plug the toothed holes with wax paper so it won't take on any more water. To sink into the earth is a gift. When I return, my son's light is blaring through dark hours. Why do we grow up thinking that light will save us? A kind of holiness ruptured. I feel my bones best when unlit. But Hortensia, here you are. Candle wick. Iridescence in my marrow. Oncoming headlights miles through the Joshua trees, sprinklers endlessly chuffing their deep clotted roots. Saying *god, god, god.*

* Title is a phrase from Paul H. Peterson, "The Mormon Reformation of 1856–1857: The Rhetoric and the Reality," *Journal of Mormon History*, Vol. 15 (1989)

NAUVOO, INTERIOR TEMPLE BURNED BY AN ARSONIST—1846

You come from my father's side of the bed. Church-good. Saintly as stink beetles that cross the burning pavement, slow. We don't mind the burning, do we. I speak to the you who is a part of me. Maybe I will find a molecule of redemption. A hairline of sanctity. Beauty that hasn't been scaled or bone-thinned. A white church in a field of ether. I drove through a cloud today, it clung to the junipers like a cerecloth, dulled the mountains in tight. If that isn't grace, tell me Hortensia, which part of my body can still be forgiven? I am growing my hair longer than our bloodline. I am braiding it as a rope to reach you.

SALVATION

I look for your replies in the lace dress that hangs like a sad
body in the back of my closet. All pearls and frass the color of
sand. But you are vasculature. Ink well. Insistence.

How tightly you must have held god between your teeth, to
stop dry-socket. Rot.

HOW TO DESCRIBE WINTER

I would rather say *biting* than *barren*. That makes me a different kind of woman. The tea kettle I inherited doesn't whistle. I'm prone to hold warnings as predictions. Bleak. The Farmer's Almanac says *on schedule*. The doctor says *your chances are below zero*. Last season, I snapped a shovel trying to shift such weight. A splinter of wood embedded deep in my thumb. Made a mound of pain. This year I am hungered down to bones. Fireside. Flannel. Severe.

WATCHING THE PRAIRIE FIRES
AS PASTIME

Regret is a scratch of light between trees, that when I get close, bleeds the margins. We think of confession differently. I have made you real in these poems, the way you made god with your prayers.

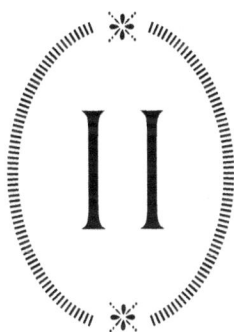

HAVE YOU COVETED ANYTHING NOT YOUR OWN?

For you, was it always Lucius, steady as a grandfather clock? His barrelhouse hands, quarry lips. Or, was there a splinter of want that flurried your sleep?

Crows cluster pools of rain on the road, flick at the last second, careless of an oncoming wreck. Or, maybe they know just when. A split glance—blink then sway. If you know where to fasten your gaze. A button has four holes to attach to the heaviest fabric. He fumbled ever so briefly. An earthquake I'll never steady.

OTHERWISE

A friend asks, how are you doing *otherwise?* Jalapeños wilted
on the counter. Sugar ants dotting the floor. I change the
dingy flower-water, wipe dog piss that rises like anger and
fouls the house. *Otherwise.* If you google dissatisfaction +
women you can find ways to hate the sheer weight of being.
While I'm told that a bone-protruding body is a lovely thing
to behold, I'd rather have exercises for shedding the pounds
of emotional labor. Besides, I need to be able to hold my
son—grown too-large for my lap, after his brain seizes and
tocks into sadness. When he was born, everyone told me
to sleep while he sleeps. Maybe that is where I lost my own
dreams. *Otherwise.* I overhear a man at the coffee shop say, *it
doesn't make sense, having this much control over my own happiness.*
I have learned the trick for lightening stains from every shape
so that you would never know it was ever there. Hortensia,
I fill your nightgown like smoke.

WINTER

I was told to never write about the moon, so I'm calling it winter, a gunshot of hours, a boarded house in the woods, cicada bodies sleepless in their transparency, their shed. I sweep them under floorboards. Burial is a crosshatch of dirt over dreams. I pretend I am sleeping under animal skin even though I'm squeamish at the sound of twigs snapping. A marching band. I tried, for a whole year, to avoid every living thing along the path. Then love. A heavy shoe. A flannel shirt over a chair. I watched him shave, the blade—a moon. Glint. Dying grass. A soda can crushed in an empty room. Sweet rust, the brocade of it, tempting every thing I taste to wisp, webs strung high in the corners. This bow. This violin light.

EXODUS

Milk froths over, feathery in a glazed mug. I watch a woodpecker forget the geography of air—churn in the invisible. Then flee. I feel silence to mean what's missing, never shapeless. Some days love. Another round of snow arriving, another mistake I'll settle into as understanding more about what I've become. I am looking for the word that falls between almost and touch. That consideration. It has its own airspace. The gap where the juniper was chopped is a frame now. If only the light would enter, I could trick myself into believing it was heat.

PORTRAITURE: DARK ROOM, SELF IN THE MIRROR

When the doctor asked about the abyss I feel in my bones, I showed him a box of bent wires stripped from the radio so he'd understand why I couldn't echolocate. I stopped drinking to trap the words. Built birdbaths around the yard for ravens. If they agreed to carry chimes on their wings would the world sound like a universal church? The only color I can't hear the music of is eggshell. I paint my eyes blue again. My first child sucked the color clean, took that brightness for himself. Now they are the first evening hour, a glass forgotten in the sink.

LOVE,

There are things I want to tell you, still. How my interior is un-churched, crocheted with mutable light, a stammer of mildew, a kind of guilt. *Come closer*, melancholia said. Sugar-throated, glimmering. See how a storm camouflages its center, the way he says my name, how it recoils in his throat, holds me captive. The way the wind is tongue-tied at the mountain base. The way the details tender over time.

EYE, BARB, THROAT, GAP

Would it be fair to say that the body is a causeway, an agenda
of leaving at low tide. Leaving always. I've come to worship
at the wrong house, again. Too many mirrors. Desire doesn't
like its reflection, the way it shimmers. A tell. The way he
said, *there's something going on with you,* and we both meant *him.*
Some fishermen can't help but cut the eyes out after the reel
and pummel. A facsimile of clouds as cornea. Burst from being
drawn to the surface. What happens when light reaches the
unsayable, the phantom pain of the hook. *There's something.*
Water isn't a safe keeper, unless what you are offering is meant
for the dark.

THE DAY A BIRD FELL DEAD AT MY FEET

And now this. Ungiving cold, in my hand. I could postpone, freeze it. Saran wrap it saintly. Or, I could can use my teeth to steady a flashlight and claw through dark, ask whatever I find beneath the ground for rest.

INHERITANCE

Snow-morning and a buck pads fresh tracks, scans the air with its wide eyes while the dogs wild. I watch it startle, stiffen its ears, then still. I've read that deer use their whole bodies to communicate, warn members of their family. This one studies the distance between my camera and its breath. A caesura. Just the other day I said *I feel dead inside*, as in the feeling of not-feeling. As if I could hold the entirety of *nothing* in my bones. Measure it the way that black paint inks into the dry cracks along my hands, thins a map. The road out, before the plows arrive, stays slicked. I embrace every precaution to stay alive. To be a good ancestor. A friend's grandmother passed and I was gifted her boxes of tiny Christmas houses, porcelain lit with glass bulbs—their windows and staged people occupy a kind of joy I can plug in. I know aloneness in that I've known its absence. What follows.

THINGS THAT MEAN LOVE, BUT MIGHT OTHERWISE GO UNMENTIONED

The sounds my neighbor makes in his woodshed, with a fresh blade. Blue jays, out of season, flushing from a tree. A campout of ravens by the trashcan, their oil-slick feathers, the very definition of beauty. The old-timey cap on the hipster who works at the drive-up liquor, the records he recommends that are impossible to find. Candles that smell like olives and atomic sunbursts. The tiniest spider that tried to hide on a painting, the one I saved with a pink cup, but then made that cup its home. The incomplete sigh when he reaches between my legs, as if he is hoarding a fraction of that pleasure. The smoke that corsets the mountains after a prescribed burn. The inexactness of light through a pile of broken windows. The rotted piano with stuck keys. His body's signature that rises to the skin, stains my hands blue. The November firepit crumpled with crosswords & comics. Honeyed whiskey on cold lips. The way he says *wolf*, without the *l*, so that his dog thinks he is barking. My dream that zombies are biting into his shoulder & my refusal to kill him when he turns.

HALF STEP

A friend digs bones of what she's loved and packs them with her each move. Between the draperies and wedding dishes. I spread ash over the ice for traction. Such terrible beauty. My husband can't name the feeling that clamps joy. But I am easy with the language of grief, the insistence of ghosts that reside in street lights and backdoor steam from the take-out place on 5th. A dog's throated bark. A necklace slipped unnoticed, lost. Maybe this is why I write to you, keeper of what I've prescribed to hold meaning. Namely, desire. Which is mostly accidental. It's pronouncement of nerves and muscles between collarbone and rib. Between A sharp and B.

VENERATION

I woke too early, painted your portrait with coffee grounds, watched the falling snow heavy the trees until they looked like old men bending at the base of the mountain in worship. I collect the scripture of bone scans and MRI's. Ache under a heating pad until it burns. Find god in the moments after a surge of pain that drops me—not yet relief, but near. When you were scared of the dark did you sing for him, to conjure heat? Were you distraught the only counter was silence? The blanket I left to dry on the porch holds the shape of a body. The architecture of a ghost. I undress in dark rooms. A single grain of sand. Faith has always been my body pressing hard against glass. Worn down by beating against the shore until it becomes something else.

DIVINING ROD

A hairline fracture. A lyre snake bedded in my underwear drawer. Curdled dream. Blade snapped from the handle. Hortensia, teach me how to read the signs—before dawn, I stumbled onto antlers shed well before March. They grew behind its body, closest to god. I know things and not—that honeycomb sealed in a jar can last a year, at best. That the river can run itself backwards. It takes a natural disaster. What would you do? Did you know that the stillest waters can secret whirlpools? The downdraft happens when bodies collide. A maelstrom. The way he cupped my chin—asked me to look— was not *at*, but *through*. As if there was a way out.

BACKSTITCH

Rub of lemon rind behind my ear to ward off insincerity. Salt tucked behind my bottom lip holds my silhouette in another's dreams. I cross traffic right foot first. Leave the ravens trinkets that splash light. These prayers, immutable. These days, a thorn in the wool. A rift.

RELIGION

Waiting for water to boil, I paint a bird with bloody talons. The clockwork of hunger. When you were faced with more survival than ornament, was there a thicker pinch of god in your hymns? Did you let the man with the meatiest hand measure? Tear the warm bread, dip into the throat of butter. I'm learning how to smudge the edges so it looks like flight. All of our rags are stained. The edges of my mouth and fingertips. We gather at our table, bless a meal. The snow settles, exhausted, as if it spent all night guarding a nest that, in the morning, proves empty.

ETERNAL REWARD

My son's tooth cracked from impact, the root—dead. When it slips from the gumline, the dentist wedges it back into place, says *we'll see if it takes*. Did you dream of me as a simple someday? A continuation of yourself? They had to cement and wire the tooth to give it a fighting chance. They built it a cage of encouragement. Stay. I fold the laundry, put dishes into their prescribed places. Cross off the litany of tasks one by one until the paper is past tense. You carried the water, chopped the wood. *Let's see if it takes.* The work of what holds me here is never done. Tomorrow, again.

HARMONICS

I am made of cyan, a riverbend at dusk, my shoes kicked free into a field that golds by the hour. The line of horizon, jagged, but only after the harvest. Winter hacked to the roots. Morning unexplained. Desire, a cut below my shoulder blade that grudges, refuses to heal. The argument that A minor makes of everything. The slant of cursive in your letters that lean toward god. A love poem. A sanctuary of blue. Veins that rise along rough hands. The rivalry between ease and the way one goes about unmaking a whole life. The testimony of wreckage, beautiful.

BAPTISM

My son buries a pinecone, hopes for a tree. But when I investigate, the instructions require a different process—after soaking, seal the seeds in a plastic bag, freeze for three months. Rehome in a mud pot. Have I mistaken god in everything? When our pond freezes, the fish go quiet. Burrow into the soft sediment. Shift only when the light breaks the veil. We leave them alone through the wide-stretch of winter—half-awake, shimmering.

"THE FEMALE RELIEF SOCIETY
OF NAUVOO"

The wind crams through the trees, claws window frames. Neighbors complain it's a bone chill, the smoke from every fireplace feeds the air thick. When narrowed down to the bone, I am most you, or most me. I am supposed to start this year right, but surgeons are slicing parts of me out early. Making room. I think of it like a secret dresser in my body, where I'll collect the raven's caw, leaves weathered down to lace, horsehair shivered free from a bow. I'll try and hold you there too—harbinger, flume, bloodline. Together, we'll wait for the salve of spring. How it ordains everything lucent. Maybe even what was cut out.

REVISION

The great saints were painted thick, layered gold. Impasto. But women's voices weren't allowed to blaze that bright. I am coming into my own story through yours. A brushstroke or two. The impact of choice. Hortensia, I have been pacing the rooms of this house for days trying to find the perfect light. I wasn't lying when I said that maybe the only thing that matters is what comes after the last word.

ACKNOWLEDGMENTS

I would like to extend gratitude to the editors and venues who first published versions of these poems.

✳

"A House of Manifestos" · *Bracken Magazine*, May 2020

"Dear Hortensia," · *Border Crossing*, Volume 13, Fall 2023

"Eye, Barb, Throat, Gap" · *Five Points*, Forthcoming

"Everyday I draw a different bird," · *Bear Review*, Volume 7.1, October 2020, Michelle Boisseau Poetry Prize Winner

"Exodus" · *CALYX*, Volume 34:1, Summer/Fall 2023

"Half Step" · *Bodega*, Volume 130, October 2023

"Have you branded an animal that you did not know to be your own?" · *Border Crossing*, Volume 13, Fall 2023

"Portraiture: Dark Room, Self in the Mirror" · *Cider Press Review*, Volume 24.3, August 2022

"Portraiture: Nude" · *Diode*, April 2022

"Putting My Dead Mom's Dog to Sleep" · *Subnivian*, Volume One, October 2020

"Sealing" · *Birdcoat Quarterly*, Issue 13, Spring 2023

"Self-Portrait as a Burned-Out Porch Light" · *Barzakh Magazine*, Spring 2021

"Subjects to Consider for Both Painting & Writing" · *Psaltery & Lyre*, December 2022

"They Promised That you Were Set Apart for Something Holy" · *Birdcoat Quarterly*, Issue 13, Spring 2023

"Things That Mean Love, but Might Otherwise Go Unmentioned" · *West Trade Review*, 2022

"Veneration" · *CALYX*, Volume 34:1, Summer/Fall 2023

"Winter" · *Reed Magazine*, Issue 154, Edwin Markam Prize Finalist

MEGAN MERCHANT (she/her)

is the owner of the editing, manuscript consultation, and mentoring business Shiversong (*www.shiversong.com*) and holds an M.F.A. degree in International Creative Writing from UNLV. She is a visual artist and the author of three full-length poetry collections with Glass Lyre Press: *Gravel Ghosts* (2016), *The Dark's Humming* (2015 Lyrebird Award), *Grief Flowers* (2018), four chapbooks, and a children's book, *These Words I Shaped for You* (Penguin Random House). Her book, *Before the Fevered Snow*, was released in April 2020 with Stillhouse Press (*NYT* New & Noteworthy). She was awarded the 2016-2017 COG Literary Award, judged by Juan Felipe Herrera, the 2018 Beullah Rose Poetry Prize, second place in the Pablo Neruda Prize for Poetry, the Inaugural Michelle Boisseau Prize, and, most recently, the New American Poetry Prize. She is the Editor of *Pirene's Fountain*. You can find her poetry and artwork at *meganmerchant.wix.com*.